'Know the Game' Series
SWIMMING

CONTENTS

FOREWORD 2	STARTING DIVE . . . 14
EARLY TRAINING AT HOME . 3	BACK CRAWL 16
AT THE SWIMMING BATHS . 4	SIMPLE BACK CRAWL TURN . 18
UNDERWATER EXERCISES . . 5	BREAST STROKE . . . 20
SIMPLE GLIDING EXERCISES . 6	DOLPHIN BUTTERFLY STROKE . 22
THE CRAWL STROKE . . 8	SWIMMING TO SURVIVE . . 24
FRONT CRAWL PRACTICES . 9	SURVIVAL AWARDS . . 30
FRONT CRAWL SEQUENCE . 10	AMATEUR SWIMMING ASSOCIATION . . . 31
FRONT CRAWL TURN — THE THROW AWAY . . . 12	
LEARNING TO ENTER THE WATER 14	SELECTED SWIMMING LAWS . 32

Printed in Great Britain by Dixon & Stell Ltd., Cross Hills, Nr. Keighley, Yorks.

FOREWORD

It is most desirable that young children get to love the water as a preliminary to learning to swim. This illustrated book stresses this as a first step, and shows how it can be achieved with simple exercises both at home and at the swimming baths, using a child's natural ability to float.

Once confidence has been gained, instruction in the strokes can begin. The authors clearly indicate by word and by diagram the technique of the front crawl, the fastest known swimming stroke. The other major strokes are also dealt with in this book, together with simple turns. There is basic instruction in Survival Swimming and a resumé of the laws governing competitive swimming. This booklet was originally written for the Amateur Swimming Association by Messrs. L. H. Koskie, M. Madders and K. B. Martin, and revised for a second edition by Colonel W. Atherton. This edition has been compiled by Miss H. J. Elkington and Messrs. C. P. Parkin and D. G. P. Smith in collaboration with the A.S.A. Education Committee. The Association is most grateful for their services.

I commend this book to all those who want their children to learn to swim and swim correctly, and to those who can already swim, but who want to acquire the correct technique associated with modern strokes.

County Alderman H. E. Fern, C.B.E., J.P.
Hon. Secretary, Amateur Swimming Association.

Early Training at Home

It is never too early to learn to swim, and the best way is the 'play-way' with baby in his bath.

Bath time should be enjoyable.

When baby becomes a toddler he can find his own exercises in the bath on his front or back. He will begin to feel even more the support of the water. A toddler enjoys blowing bubbles under the water and looking for fishes. These are both good exercises for getting used to the water.

Encourage baby to enjoy bouncing in water and show no concern if baby's face gets wet.

At the Swimming Baths

One of the best ways of establishing confidence is to get the youngster moving through the water, on his front or back.

By using artificial aids to buoyancy and kicking his legs, he can experience this thrill even during his first visit to the baths.

Don't rush the youngster into the water; before undressing him, take him to see mother and father swim, or even an older brother who can already move through the water, and even then don't hurry him. Wait until he seems to want to go in. Let him learn because he wants to.

Underwater Exercises

To do a hand stand take a deep breath, jump off the bottom of the bath and keep your head down, turning your body to jump on to your hands. Practise until you can hold the position quite steadily.

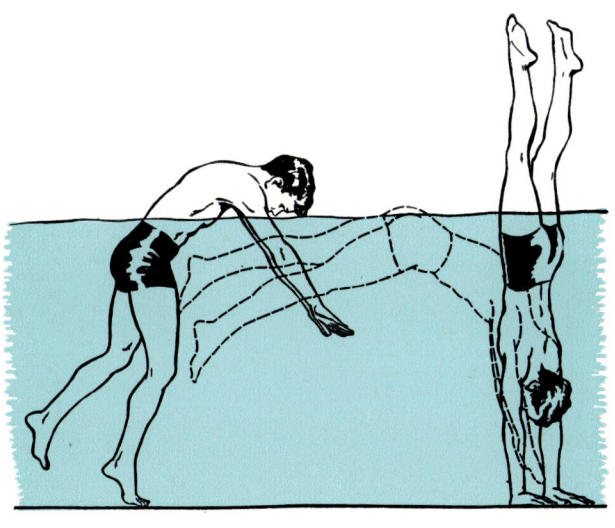

Push from the side, keep your head down and try swimming between somebody's legs. Keep your eyes open so that you can see where you are going. All good swimmers should be able to keep their eyes open under water.

Simple Gliding Exercises

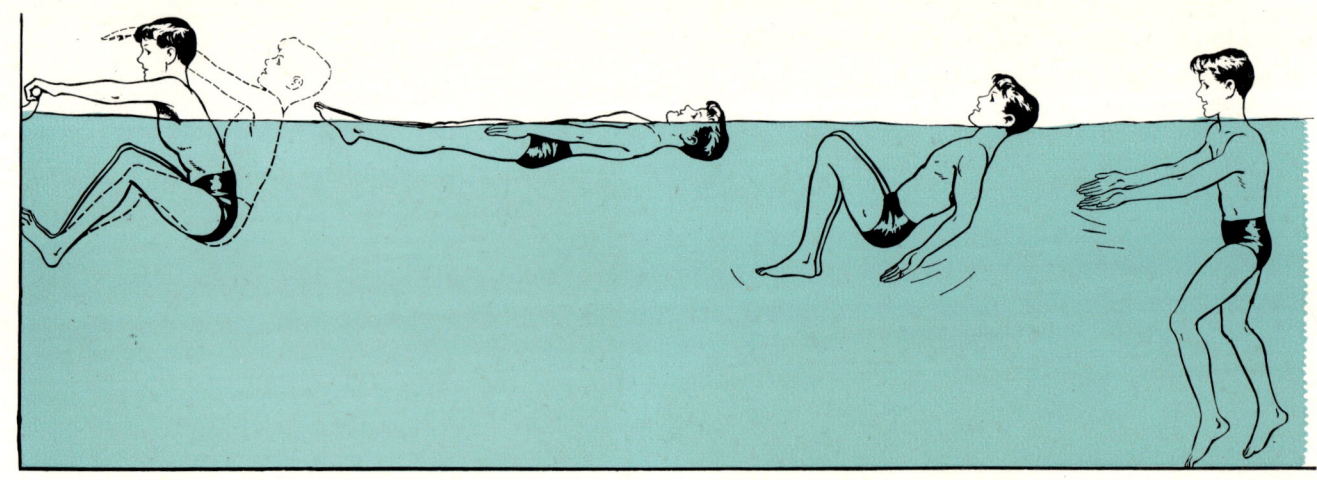

As the child progresses the need for aids will become less and less until he can move through the water entirely unaided.

Pushing away from the side of the bath while floating on the back is good practice for learning the back crawl.

Standing up again from the floating position on your back is very important and must be learnt as soon as possible. Make an attempt to 'sit down' and at the same time push forward with your hands.

The gliding exercise shown here is a very important one. To 'keep going' along the water surface is one of the first big steps in learning to swim.

Some people find it very easy to stand up again, but if you do not, the pictures below show you how to do it.

Getting on your feet again from the gliding position, face downwards, must be learnt as soon as possible. Use your hands as well as your feet in getting your balance.

The Crawl Stroke

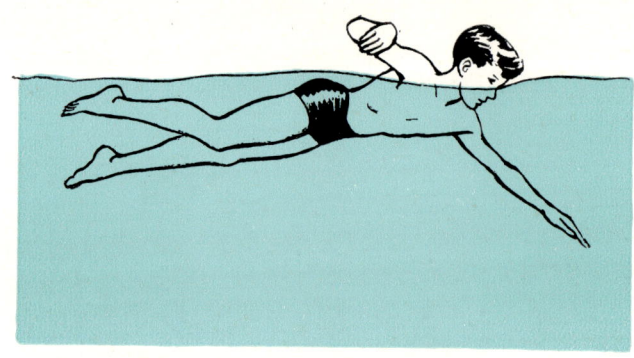

To move effectively through water by any stroke the body must be as streamlined as possible.

In the crawl stroke the body should lie as straight and as horizontal as possible along the surface of the water. The head is held comfortably so that the water is at the top of the forehead, the eyes looking forward or slightly downward. It is important to keep this horizontal position, with the spine straight. Twisting and rolling should be avoided, as this means energy wasted.

The arm action of the stroke is alternately pulling under the water and recovering over the water. Most of the propulsive power comes from the arm action. The legs, by keeping up a steady beat, give balance and poise to the body and are a further aid to this driving power.

It is essential to have an efficient leg action before the crawl stroke can be swum properly. This leg action stabilises the body and allows the arms to work effectively.

In order to breathe, the head should be turned to one side in such a way that the rhythm of the stroke is not disturbed.

These things (leg and arm movements), can be practised separately, as shown on the next page.

Front Crawl Practices

Leg Action

Grasp the rail. Work your legs up and down with an easy swing from the hips. Let the whole of your leg be as loose as possible. Keep the legs close together and see that only the heels break the water surface.

Practise the kick at varying speeds. Slowly at first, dropping down to about 18 ins., then quicken up, with a shallower drive. Try to make the movement start from your hips and ripple down your legs, finishing with a 'whip-lash' effect with the feet. Get moving as soon as possible by using a float.

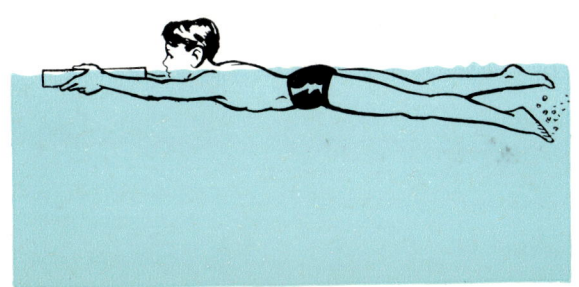

Arm Action

Arm work for the crawl should be practised in shallow water at first.

Stand in the water. Lean forward with shoulders submerged. Start with one arm forward, slightly bent so that your hand is in front of your shoulder and just under the water. The other arm should be at the side and pressed against the thigh. Press down under your body with the forward arm, and back to brush your thigh. At the same time bend and lift the other elbow so that the hand is clear of the water and move it forward to the starting position.

Continue the action, one arm pulling as the other lifts and swings forward, keeping your shoulders square.

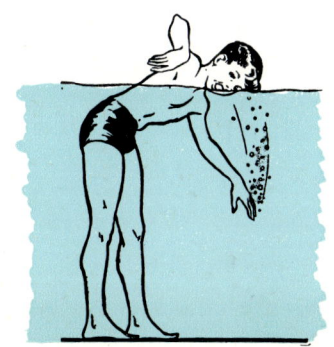

Front Crawl Sequence

The arm pull starts with the slightly cupped hand sliding forward in an easy reach position. It is then pulled downward under the water level, with the arm almost straight until the hand is below the centre of the body.

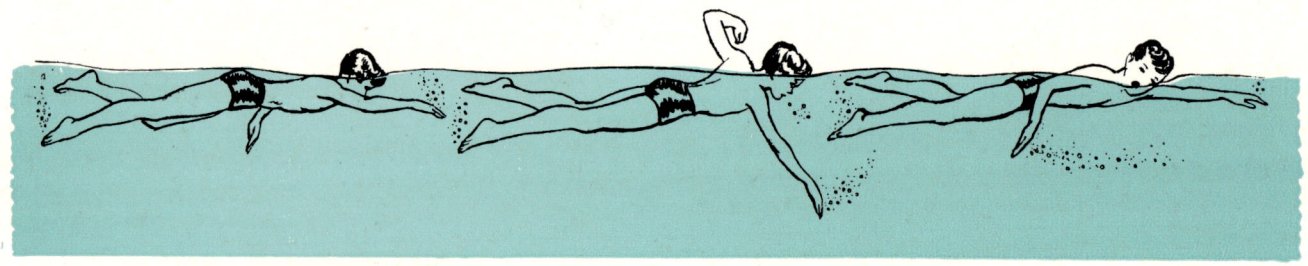

The pull is continued backward until the thumb reaches the thigh. The arm is then recovered from the water. At this stage the other arm has just entered the water to commence pulling.

The arm leaving the water is brought out elbow first, with a sharp movement, forearm and wrist relaxed. The elbow comes over in an arc and the forearm continues forward, the hand entering the water thumb first, between centre line and shoulder line. The whole arm has now completed its stroke and the sequence is repeated.

The legs work close together as in a horizontal walking position but with this difference: the movement starts at the hip and travels **down** the whole leg as a continuous wave, finishing with a **whip-lash** action at the foot.

In order to achieve this the whole leg, and especially the ankle, must be relaxed. On this downward wave the knees should not sink lower than shown in the illustrations.

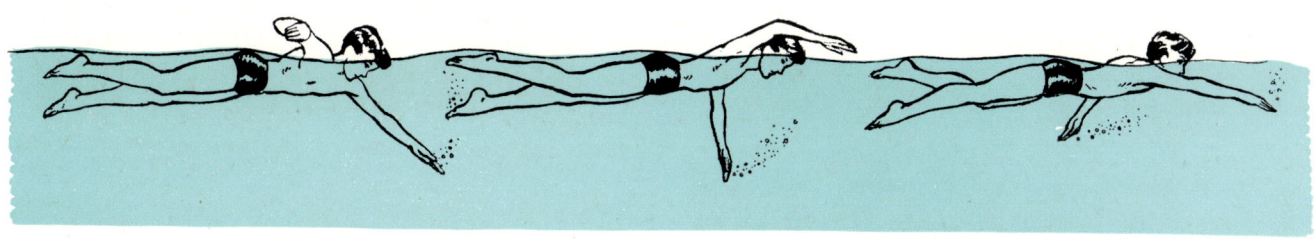

The head is turned sideways as the arm at that side starts to recover and is 'pillowed' against the water during inhalation. (If explosive breathing is used both exhalation and inhalation take place.) The smooth speed of an experienced swimmer creates a trough in the water behind the bow wave, thus giving the impression, as he turns his head to breathe, of inhaling below the water surface.

Immediately afterwards the head turns face downwards for exhalation as the other arm is recovered. The aim is to disturb the body poise as little as possible.

Some people breathe in and out while the mouth is clear of the water; this is probably the most natural method for this stroke. Others breathe **in** while the mouth is clear and breathe **out** into the water.

Front Crawl Turn—The Throw Away

This is one of the simplest turns.

The swimmer should approach the wall closely, without any reduction of speed, and touch with one hand. As soon as this is done the body should be **tucked** up and turned on to the side of the touching hand. The head rises out of the water and the feet sink. The free arm makes a scooping movement to help the body round and to keep it close to the wall as it turns chest downwards. At the same time the touching arm leaves the wall and is thrown over the head. The knees should be bent and the feet, slightly apart, pressed firmly against the wall.

As the swimmer drives powerfully away from the wall the head should be between the arms. The body now glides under the water, absolutely straight. As the speed of the drive slackens, the leg action should start. Then one arm starts to pull, bringing the swimmer back to the surface when the full stroke begins again.

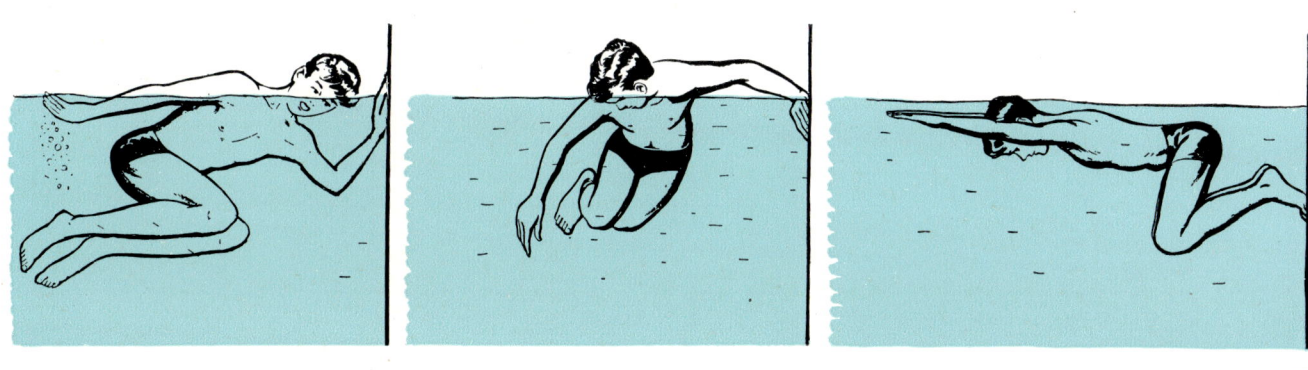

Learning to Enter the Water

Learn in stages.
1. Push out over the water from the top step in the shallow end. Keep your head down and try to go under the water.

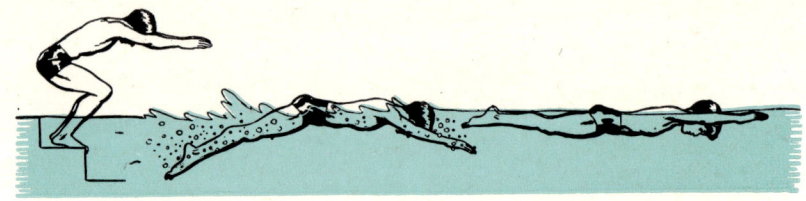

Starting Dive
Front Crawl

Your name will be called and your starting place indicated. When the starter says 'Take your marks' you assume the position shown in Fig. 1. When all the competitors are steady he will give the signal to start.

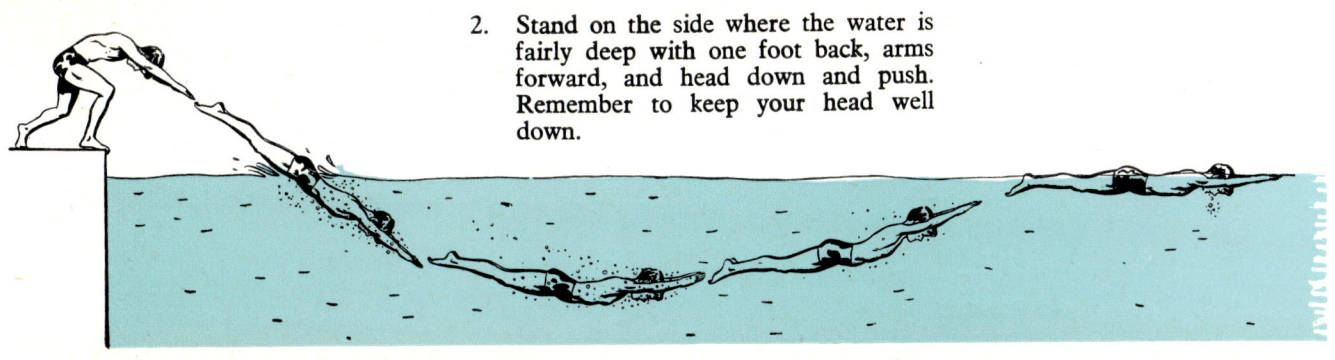

2. Stand on the side where the water is fairly deep with one foot back, arms forward, and head down and push. Remember to keep your head well down.

On hearing the signal, allow yourself to fall forward and, as you overbalance, hurl yourself out over the water (Figs. 2 and 3). Your entry should not be flat and do not slap the water with your hands or start your legs kicking in the air. Dive about two feet down under the surface (Fig. 4) and glide, then pull with one arm and start your legs going (Fig. 5).

You must reach the surface before you need to recover your arm, turn your head sideways to breathe and start swimming fast (Fig. 6). Everything must be done as smoothly as possible.

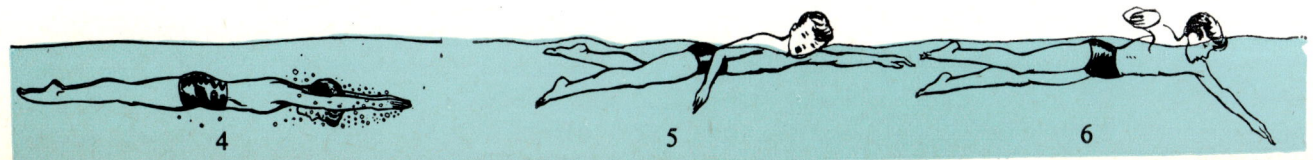

Page fifteen

Back Crawl

Starting a race

All back stroke swimming races are started in the water. The starter will ask you to get in the water and give you your place. He will then tell you to 'Take your marks'. Get hold of the rail, tuck up and put your feet against the wall—but notice that your feet must be below the surface of the water. When everybody is quite still he will give the signal to start.

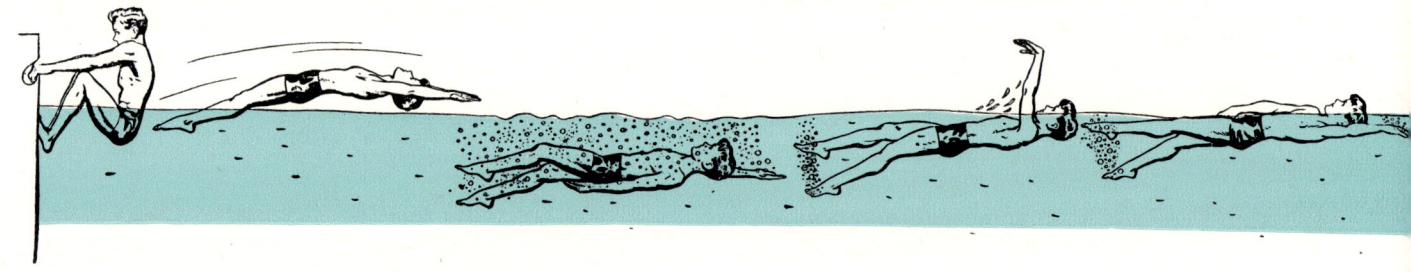

The arm action operates continuously without pause. The hand enters the water, little finger first. The arm follows and starts the pull with a sideways movement, the hand slightly bent on the forearm but vertical to the surface like the blade of an oar. The pull is continued into a push until the hand touches the side of the thigh.

The other arm has begun its pull so that the movement is continuous. The recovering arm is brought out of the water and swung backward, straight but relaxed.

The body should be horizontal, with the hips slightly below the surface. The head is comfortably 'pillowed' on the water and the face is clear of the water with the ears

Throw yourself out over the surface of the water as far as you can. Hollow your back and throw your head back. Glide under water 2 ft. below the surface until the speed of the dive drops away and then pull with one arm first and start your legs going.

Come to the surface before you need to recover that arm and start swimming fast. Everything must be done smoothly.

just below the surface. The eyes will usually be looking upwards or slightly towards the feet. The shoulders should be level, the back straight and the body as a whole relaxed.

In this stroke the mouth and nose should be clear of the water, which allows breathing to take place almost naturally.

There are usually six legs beats to one complete arm cycle. The leg movement is similar to that of the front crawl except that there should be a slight inward rotation of the legs, which, with the foot movements from the 'loose' ankles, produces a whipping action. Only the toes should reach the water surface. The emphasis of the kick should be on the upward movement. The knees should not break the surface as this will slow down the forward movement.

Simple Back Crawl Turn

Swim in fast and **remain on the back until the foremost hand has touched the end of the bath.** As soon as this happens the knees are bent into a 'tuck' position with the head raised, remembering to get as close to the wall as possible. The feet will sink and the body rotates towards the touching hand, assisted by the other hand pulling round in the water. This should bring the feet into the position where they are pressed firmly against the wall. The body will have sunk slightly in the water and the arms are placed beyond the head while a strong push-off is made from the side. The glide is held until the speed begins to diminish; then the leg action is recommenced. As the body comes up to the surface, one arm pulls as in the start and the full stroke is continued.

1

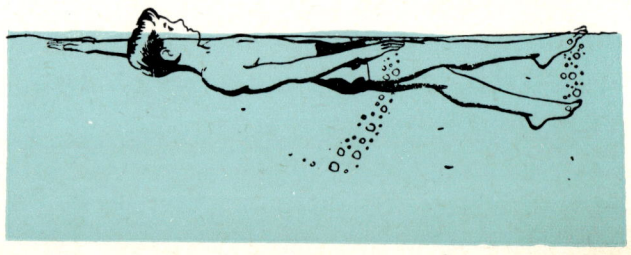

7

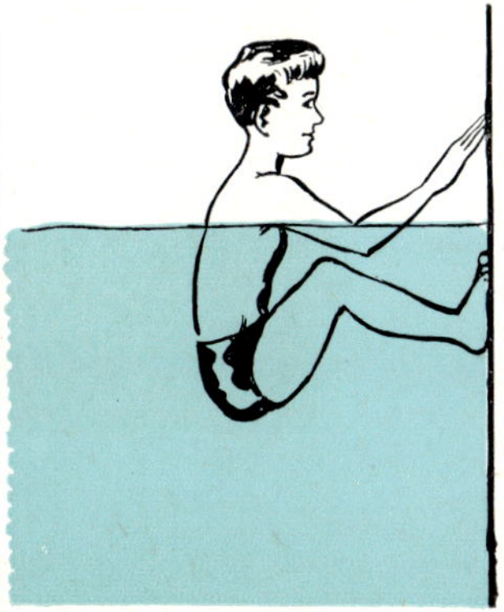

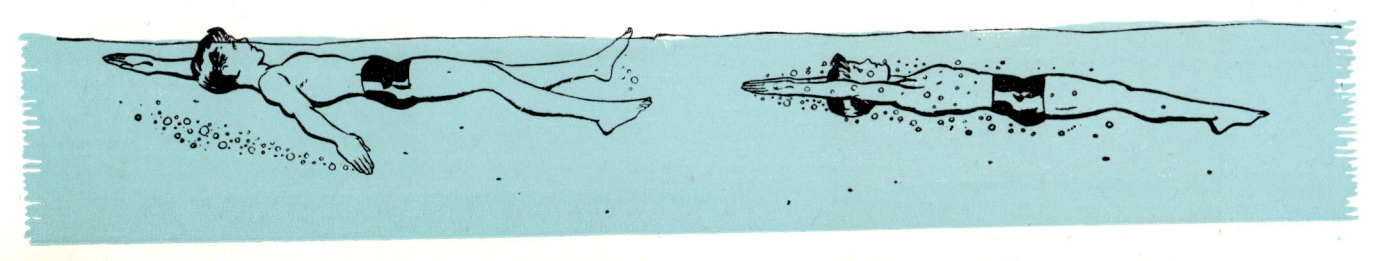

Breast Stroke

The breast stroke is quite different from the crawl in its movements. Both arms make their stroke together and the legs swirl round simultaneously and symmetrically, not beating alternately as in the crawl. You will therefore need to practise arm and leg strokes separately before starting on the stroke as a whole. These exercises in the water are suggested to get you accustomed to this new stroke.

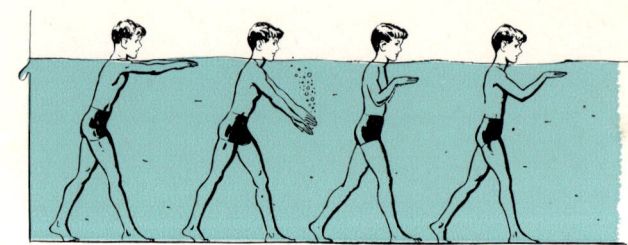

Practising the arm stroke

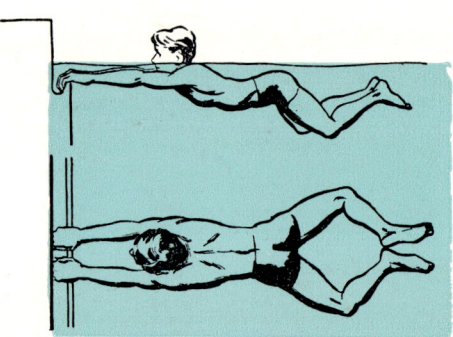

Practising the leg stoke

The body should be almost parallel to the surface of the water, with the legs a little lower than the head, which is slightly raised. The shoulders should be in line with the water surface and must be kept level. The eyes look ahead along or just under the surface of the water. To commence the arms are straight in front, without tension, hands together with thumbs touching, slightly cupped, with palms down. Again, without tension, the legs should trail together, straight, with toes pointing backward and the soles uppermost.

The arm pull and leg kick are inter-timed; first the arms pull, whilst the legs remain together and streamlined, then, as the arms are recovering, the legs make their kick.

The arms pull together with a downward-sideways movement, continuing until the angle between them is **rather less than a right angle.** Do not pull your arms wider than this.

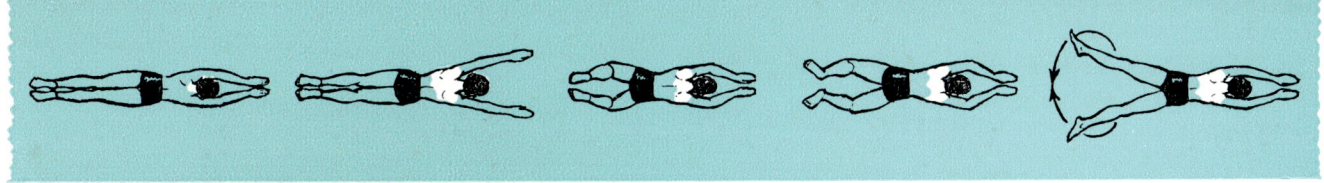

At this point the hands are about twelve inches below the water level — without pause the elbows bend, the arms swing together and the hands make a swirling movement which brings them together palms downward — ready to move forward to the starting position — where the arms are extended, once more, without strain, just below the surface.

Leg movements must also be symmetrical and simultaneous. From the extended 'trailing' position the feet are drawn well up towards the seat and the knees move forward and outward. (There should be no strain in this position.) Continuing without pause the knees part slightly and the toes are drawn towards the shins — then with the utmost vigour the feet move outward and backward bringing the legs round in an outward sweep until they come together again with ankles touching and toes pointing backward.

Inhalation, which is quick and deep through the mouth, takes place just before the arms reach the deepest part of the pull.

The rhythm of the breast stroke depends on the correct timing of the leg kicks and arm pulls and also the breathing; once these are synchronised there will be a gliding phase in the stroke every time the body straightens.

Dolphin Butterfly Stroke

The Dolphin Butterfly is the youngest of the recognised strokes. At first it was swum as a kind of breast stroke but the two strokes became separated in 1953. It is a difficult stroke for beginners but can be learnt as soon as you are a good crawl swimmer.

Arms

The arms enter the water between shoulder and centre line, hands downward. They are then pulled downward and backward, in a similar way to the front crawl stroke, until they are in line with the hips. The arms are now lifted clear of the water and thrown vigorously forward to the point of entry. The arms, with fingers loose, should be low over the water but clear of it. Towards the end of the pull the elbows begin to bend and they reach the water surface first.

Legs

In the same way as the crawl leg kick, the Dolphin Butterfly leg movement begins in the hips and moves all the way down the leg to the toes. However, in the Dolphin kick, the legs move at the same time (not alternately), and there is more movement from the hips and knees.

Firstly the legs move upwards together. During this movement the knees should begin to bend and part. When the feet are just below the surface the knees are straightened quickly and the legs brought down vigorously. This leg beat is usually performed twice while the arms are making one stroke.

Breathing

Breathing in this stroke takes place after the arm pull and the second downbeat of the legs. This brings the mouth clear of the water.

The breath can be taken with the head looking forward, as in the breast stroke, or turned sideways, as in the crawl stroke. Most swimmers prefer to use explosive breathing for this stroke, breathing out and then in again while the mouth is clear of the water.

Swimming to Survive

One of the most important reasons for learning to swim is that it enables you to learn how to save yourself if you get into difficulties in water. There is a great deal more to saving yourself than just swimming; numerous other skills have to be learned if you are to be able to deal with almost any problem with which you may be faced. These skills are called 'Survival Swimming'.

Firstly you must learn to be a good swimmer, not just a length of the bath but at least a quarter of a mile. Try swimming with clothing on and at speed. In an emergency you may well be in water in your clothes and you may well need to swim away quickly from the area of a sinking ship or to avoid falling wreckage or other people jumping in.

When you can swim well, try the skills shown on the following pages until you can perform them all. Perhaps when you have mastered them you may like to test yourself. The Amateur Swimming Association have devised tests for this purpose, with three degrees of difficulty, Bronze, Silver and Gold. Your local swimming club should be able to arrange a test for you. Many schools, also, can arrange tests for their pupils. (Details of the tests are shown on page 30.)

Safe Entry

It may be necessary to enter water from a height. Learn to do this safely. If possible step off, do not leap or throw yourself, keep body straight, head up, hands to sides.

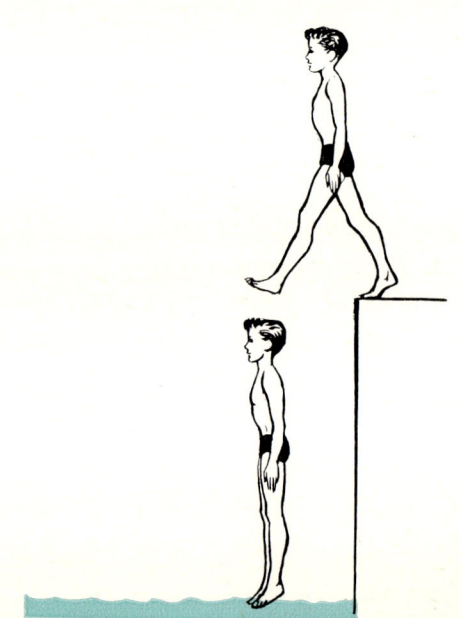

This keeps the body upright. To enter the water from a height on your back or front could cause injury. If you do not know depth of water spread your arms and legs to act as brakes. They will stop you going too deep.

Treading Water

It may be important for you to stay in one place either to size up the situation or to await rescue with a group of others. Practise treading water; most people prefer a breast stroke kick with the legs, but some prefer a crawl kick. A wavelike movement with the hands forcing down on the water helps to keep the body up. It may be necessary to keep afloat after having sustained an arm or leg injury, so practise treading water with one arm held to the side or even with both hands behind your back.

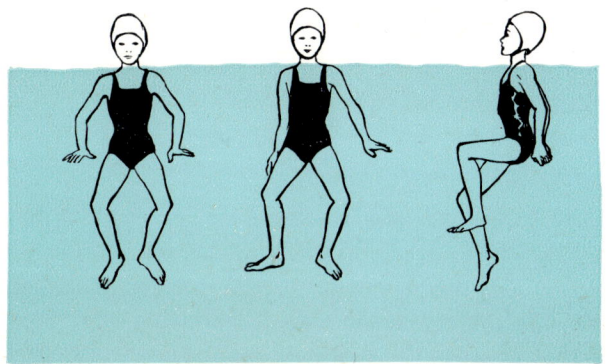

Removal of Clothing

If you are likely to be in the water for any length of time you should remove clothes which will become a hindrance to you. This needs practice. If a garment will come off 'coat style' remove it this way. If something must come off over the head roll it well up under armpits then pull over head in one quick movement. Lower garments can often be kicked or 'wriggled' off, but it is likely that the hands may have to be used. Garments which can be made into floats while being worn should of course be left on. Once off, many clothes can actually help you to float. Practise making floats from clothes as shown.

Inflation of Clothing

Trousers. Inflate by fastening front, tying a knot at the end of the legs, and then either pulling them vigorously over the head scooping in the air or blowing air up into them from under water. They can then be used either to support the legs by holding them between the ankles or to support the upper body by holding them on the chest.

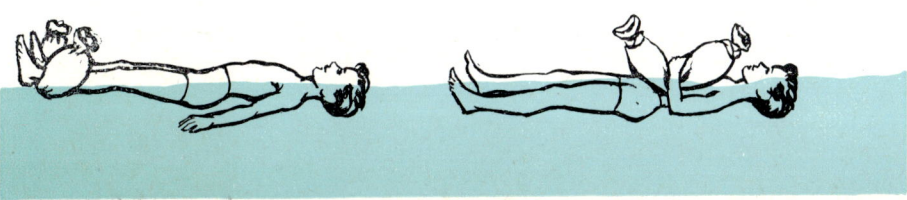

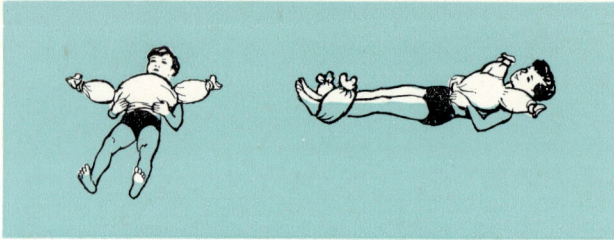

Shirts, Blouses, Skirts. Remove shirt or blouse, knot sleeves. Fasten the top button behind your neck so that the shirt is back to front. Then, lying back, scooping air into the shirt with the tail. This will inflate the body and sleeves making an effective float. This can also be combined with trousers as an ankle support. Skirts are best left on and air scooped in by holding the lower hem and scooping forward until a bubble of air forms under the front of the skirt.

Submerging

This may be necessary to swim under obstacles in the water, such as wreckage or oil, and it can be done either head first or feet first.

Head first. If you can see clearly and have plenty of room this method may be used. Push your head, body and arms down under the water, bending at the hips. Then raise the legs up above the body. The weight of the legs will drive you quite deep. If you need to go deeper use your arms and legs in a downward swimming action.

Feet first. If you have very little room or are uncertain about what is under the water, submerge feet first. This enables you to go down in a much smaller space and you are less likely to strike your head on submerged objects. This time raise the body and arms as high above the water as possible and their weight will force you down. An upward sweep of the arms when under the water can be used to drive you even deeper.

Now try swimming under the water. A short distance at first, increasing it until you feel confident you could clear most obstacles. Many swimmers use a breast stroke arm and leg action underwater, but some prefer a dog paddle arm action with a crawl type leg kick. Try them both until you find which you prefer. Finally you must be able to get out of the water. If you can reach the top of the bank it is usually a case of heaving yourself up with the arms, getting a leg over the top and clambering out. If you cannot reach the top, a good breast stroke leg kick will often raise you up enough to get a grip on the bank. If the bottom is not too deep a spring off the bottom will help.

Awards for Proficiency in Personal Survival

Applications to Miss L. V. Cook, 12 King's Avenue, Woodford Green, Essex (Buckhurst 9361) for every A.S.A. Award.

Tests and Conditions

General. The tests for each award shall be continuous, in the order set out and without pause. (If, however, the bath in which the test is taken has no facilities for Test 1 in any of the Awards, this may be performed separately at a suitable venue provided that the appropriate clothing for that Award is worn, the same examiner(s) present, and that the actual Award test begins with a jump from the highest available platform.) They must be performed in an efficient, confident, and conclusive manner and there must be no contact with the bath wall or floor at any time, even if this necessitates the candidate treading water whilst awaiting his turn to perform a test. In the distance swims, circuits rather than lengths of the bath should be swum in the tests. Costume or swimming trunks must be worn beneath all clothing, which must be clean and freshly washed.

Examiners. The examiner shall be (i) an official whose name appears on the District or County List, or (ii) a holder of the A.S.A. Teachers' Certificate, or (iii) a person approved by the A.S.A. Applications for approval should be made to the Organiser (see above). For the Gold Award, two examiners are necessary.

Bronze Award. Dress: Men and Boys in trousers and shirt, or pyjamas; Women and Girls in dress, or slacks and blouse, or pyjamas.
1. Jump from a height of not less than 6 feet.
2. Swim 50 yards.
3. Tread water for 3 minutes in a vertical position.
4. Undress in the water.
5. Swim 440 yards, surface diving once during the swim, and swimming at least 5 yards completely submerged.
6. Climb out from deep water without the use of steps or assistance. The level of water must be at least 9 inches below the landing place.

Silver Award. Dress: As for Bronze Award, with the addition of a sleeveless or short sleeved pullover.
1. Jump from a height of not less than 10 feet.
2. Swim 100 yards in less than 4 minutes.
3. Tread water for one minute in a vertical position, using legs and one arm only.
4. Tread water for three minutes in a vertical position.
5. Undress in the water and demonstrate the ability to make a float from clothing.
6. Surface dive in a depth of approximately 6 feet of water. (a) Head first and (b) feet first and swim a minimum of 5 yards completely submerged, before re-surfacing on each occasion.
7. Swim 880 yards, of which 440 yards shall be on the back and 440 yards on the front or side.
8. Climb out from deep water as for Bronze Award.

Gold Award. Dress: Men and Boys in long-sleeved shirt, trousers, pants, long-sleeved pullover, stockings or socks; Women and Girls in long-sleeved dress; skirt or slacks, and long-sleeved blouse, knickers, long-sleeved pullover, stockings or socks.
1. Jump from a height of not less than 10 feet.
2. Swim 100 yards in less than 4 minutes.
3. Tread water for 1 and a half minutes in a vertical position with hands clasped behind back.
4. Tread water for 4 minutes in a vertical position.
5. Undress in the water.
6. Make a float from clothing and use it to float for 5 minutes without use of arms or legs except when reinflating the clothing if necessary.
7. Swim 1,000 yards, surface diving during the swim 12 times head first and 12 times feet first to pass each time, head first, through a hoop, tyre or ring the top of which is at least 3 feet below the surface, in less than 30 minutes.
8. Climb out from deep water as for Bronze Award.

The Awards are open to all. The entry fee is 5/-, and successful candidates will receive an enamelled badge. Additionally, costume badges may be purchased for 5/6d. No fee is payable by a candidate who fails. If costume or replacement badges are applied for, reference to the original application or receipt number should be made. Details of awards will be recorded in a National Register of Swimmers proficient in Personal Survival.

The Amateur Swimming Association

The Amateur Swimming Association is one of the oldest governing bodies of amateur sports in this country, for it was founded as far back as 1869. On 7th January of that year, a meeting of swimmers was held at the German Gymnasium, King's Cross, London, and it was decided to form an Association under the title of the Associated Metropolitan Swimming Clubs. On 24th June, 1869, the title was changed to the London Swimming Association, and five years later (in February 1874) once more changed to the Swimming Association of Great Britain. The final change to the Amateur Swimming Association was made on 3rd March, 1886.

The Association governs amateur swimming for both sexes in England. Prior to its formation, there was little distinction between amateur and professional swimmers; the swimming baths were few, ill constructed, and badly ventilated, and sports meetings were few in number and indifferently organised. Now, nearly every city has one or more swimming baths. The Association operates through a Committee consisting of a President (changed each year), Hon. Secretary and Hon. Treasurer, together with two representatives from each of the five District Associations and a representative of the Combined Services — fourteen members in all. Advisory Committees of experts deal with matters relating to Swimming, Diving and the game of Water Polo.

On 19th July, 1908, the Association convened a meeting in London of representatives of a number of European countries, with the object of founding a World Federation to control amateur swimming. This meeting was the birth of the Federation Internationale de Natation Amateur, which has now over 80 nations affiliated. The late George Hearn (President of the A.S.A. in 1908) was the first Hon. Secretary of the Federation, and remained in that office for 20 years. The present Hon. Secretary of the A.S.A. (H. E. Fern, C.B.E., J.P.) was President from 1936 to 1948, for many years Hon. Treasurer and in 1960 was elected Honorary President for life in recognition of his services to world swimming for more than 50 years.

The A.S.A. is divided into five Districts — Midland, North, North-East, South and West — and it is to these District Associations that clubs affiliate. The rules and regulations of the A.S.A. apply in each District, supplemented by regulations peculiar to each.

The objects of the A.S.A. shall be to:

(a) Promote the teaching and practice of swimming, diving and water polo and stimulate public opinion in favour of providing proper accommodation and facilities for them.

(b) Draw up, publish and enforce uniform laws for the control and regulation of Amateur swimming, diving and water polo championships and competitions in England, and deal with any infringement thereof.

While the Association promotes and controls amateur swimming, it is also engaged on the important educational work of encouraging everyone to learn to swim, and is making every effort to ensure that the teaching of swimming shall be on the soundest lines. Its certificate of proficiency to teach modern swimming strokes has been awarded — following an examination in both theory and practice — to 16,000 individuals. There is a similar examination for teachers of diving and the Association also awards a Coaches' Certificate, which demands ability and experience of a high order. The Education Committee of the Association conducts the Teachers' Certificate Examinations, and produces text books and films on the teaching of swimming, diving and personal survival.

The A.S.A. sponsors Advanced Training Courses for swimmers and coaches each year at Loughborough College and Crystal Palace National Recreation Centre, while its National Championships, open to the world, are held at an Annual Championships Festival over a period of several days.

Selected Swimming Laws

Definition of an Amateur. *A.S.A. Law 43.*

An amateur sportsman is one who engages in sport for the pleasure and physical, mental or social benefits he derives therefrom, and to whom sport is nothing more than a recreation.

The law mentions a number of offences as a result of which anyone in swimming or any other athletic sport ceases to be an amateur. Such a person would become either (a) a professional, (b) a suspended or disqualified amateur. A professional in most other sports is inelegible to compete as an amateur swimmer. There is also a list of activities in which a swimmer may engage without endangering his amateur status.

Entry Forms. *A.S.A. Law 52.*

The copyright form of the A.S.A. shall be used for all open competitions held under A.S.A. laws. No entry shall be accepted unless it is accompanied by the entry fee and a signed declaration of amateur status. There are special conditions for handicap events.

Competitors' Costumes. *A.S.A. Law 58.*

A competitor in an event under A.S.A. laws held in the presence of both sexes shall wear:

Male. A swimming costume or trunks with slips either incorporated or separate, provided the wearing of trunks is permitted by the bath authority.

Female. A swimming costume of one piece, devoid of open work. Shoulder straps shall be attached to the main part of the costume both back and front.

The texture of costumes and trunks shall be non-transparent.

Mixed Competitions. *A.S.A. Law 55.*

A contest between the sexes shall not be permitted to take place in public. This law shall not apply to:

(a) A team race or team diving contest in which each team consists of the same number of members of each sex as each other team.

(b) A school contest confined to school children under the age of sixteen years.

Starting. *A.S.A. Law 61.*

When, as a competitor, you come under starter's orders, relax as far as possible while he is giving the necessary instructions. Stand on or near your starting point. On a signal from the referee, the competitors shall step on to the back portion of the starting block and remain there. On the preparatory command from the starter 'take your marks', the competitors shall immediately take up a starting position and when all the competitors are stationary, the starter shall give a starting signal (shot, whistle or command). The starter is required to refrain from giving the signal until all the competitors in the event are still.

In the event of a false start in a scratch race the starter is required to call back the competitors at the first or second false start and remind them of the starting procedure. When a third start is necessary, the starter shall disqualify a defaulting competitor whether he was a previous offender or not. In a handicap event, however, a competitor starting before his time is disqualified by the check starter, unless he returns to his starting place on the side of the bath or in the water under his original station and starts again.

Breast Stroke. *A.S.A. Law 66.*

(a) A competitor may start with a plunge or jump, or in the water, facing the course, and holding the rail or side of the bath or other starting place with both hands.

(b) Both hands shall be pushed forward together from the breast on or under the surface of the water and brought back simultaneously and symmetrically with lateral extension.

(c) The body shall be kept perfectly on the breast, and both shoulders in line with the surface of the water.

(d) The feet shall be drawn up together, the knees bent and open. The movements shall be continued with a rounded and outward sweep of the feet, bringing the legs together. Up and down movements of the legs in the vertical plane are prohibited. All movements of the legs and feet shall be simultaneous, symmetrical, and in the same lateral plane.

(e) When touching at the turn or on finishing a race, the touch shall be made with both hands simultaneously on the same level with shoulders in horizontal position.

(f) Swimming under the surface of the water is prohibited except one arm stroke and one leg kick after start and turn.

(g) A swimmer may take one stroke to assist him in returning promptly to the surface. Either the complete or incomplete movement of the arms and legs shall be considered as one stroke or kick. From the moment when the swimmer, after start or turn, begins the second stroke, one part of the head shall always break the surface of the water.

Butterfly Stroke. *A.S.A. Law 67.*

The rules for butterfly are similar to those for breast stroke except that in recovery both arms shall be brought forward together over the water and all movements of the legs and feet shall be executed in a simultaneous and symmetrical manner. Simultaneous up and down movements of the legs and feet in the vertical plane are permitted. After the start and at turns a swimmer is permitted one or more leg kicks and one arm pull under the water, which must bring him to the surface.

Back Stroke. *A.S.A. Law 68.*

(a) Competitors shall line up in the water facing the starting end, with both hands resting on the end or rail of the bath or course. The feet, including toes, shall be under the surface of the water. Standing in gutters is prohibited.

(b) At the signal for starting, and when turning, they shall push off and swim on their backs throughout the race.

(c) Any competitor leaving his normal position on the back before his head, foremost hand or arm has touched the end of the course for the purpose of turning or finishing shall be disqualified.

Free Style. *A.S.A. Law 65.*

A competitor may start with a plunge or jump, or in the water holding the rail or side of the bath or other starting place. A competitor may swim any style or styles and rules relating specifically to breast, butterfly, and back stroke swimming shall not apply. In turning and finishing the competitor must touch the end of the bath or course with any part of his body.

Finishing. *A.S.A. Law 59.*

Where there is a rail at the finish, the competitors must touch the wall if the course cannot otherwise be completed.

Standing. *A.S.A. Law 63.*

A competitor does not disqualify himself in a free style event by standing upon the bottom of the bath or course for the purpose of resting. N.B.—This applies to *free style only*.

Officials. *A.S.A. Law 59.*

For all open competitions (that is competitions in which members of more than one club are eligible to compete) there shall be: (a) a referee; (b) a starter; (c) a check starter for handicaps; (d) not less than two turning judges for each turn or take-over line other than the finishing line (where the place judges function); (e) not less than two placing judges, and such additional judges as may be necessary to disqualify swimmers who fail to comply with A.S.A. laws or the rules of the competition during the race; (f) a sufficient number of time-keepers to ensure that the appropriate swimmers are selected for the next round or final; (g) competitors' stewards. A decision made by the appropriate officials shall be final, but the referee shall give a decision on any point where the opinions of the judges may differ. He has authority to interfere in a competition at any stage to ensure that the racing conditions are observed.

Prizes. *A.S.A. Law 70.*

No promoter shall offer, nor competitor accept, as a prize:

(a) Money, either as a prize or in lieu of a prize.

(b) Savings Certificates or similar documents.

(c) An order for goods from a tradesman or shopkeeper.

(d) Wearing apparel, food or consumable goods. Wearing apparel does not include a swimming costume or training suit, or a tie authorised by the A.S.A., a District, County or Club.

THE SWIMMING TIMES

The world's leading swimming magazine

- SWIMMING
- DIVING
- LIFE-SAVING
- WATER POLO

Invaluable to Swimmers, Club Officials, Baths Committees and Public Libraries

It creates a new and greater interest in the sport

KEEN SWIMMERS ALL READ IT

The Swimming Times

1/9 monthly (2/3d. by post). 21s. per annum (27s. by post).   4, Waddon Park Avenue, Croydon, CR9 4AX, Surrey, England